OCTAVIA
AND OTHER POEMS

Poetry by Naomi Long Madgett:

Songs to a Phantom Nightingale (1941)
One and the Many (1956)
Star by Star (1965, 1970)
Pink Ladies in the Afternoon (1972)
Exits and Entrances (1978)
Phantom Nightingale: Juvenilia (1981)
Octavia and Other Poems (1988)

Octavia
and Other Poems

BY

Naomi Long Madgett

Illustrated by
Leisia Duskin

Chicago
THIRD WORLD PRESS
1988

Copyright © 1988
by Naomi Long Madgett

First Edition
All rights reserved

International Standard Book Number 0-883781-21-2
Library of Congress Catalog Card Number 87-51637

Printed in the United States of America

Third World Press
Post Office Box 730
Chicago, Illinois 60619

In loving memory of
Clarence Marcellus Long, Sr.
and
Kenneth Lowell Johnson, Sr.
who started me on this quest

and for
Karen Octavia Long
who carries on the name

Acknowledgements

I am most grateful to members of my family and to those persons in Guthrie, Oklahoma who were helpful in supplying information for Part I of this collection.

Some of the poems in Part II first appeared in *Argo*; *Callaloo*; *Contemporary Michigan Poetry*, Michael Delp, Conrad Hilberry, and Herbert Scott, eds., (Wayne State University Press, 1988); *Great Lakes Review; Green River Review; Michigan Quarterly Review; Obsidian; Say That the River Turns—The Impact of Gwendolyn Brooks*, Haki R. Madhubuti, ed. (Third World Press, 1987); *Woman Poet—The Midwest;* and *The Zora Neale Hurston Forum*. Permission to reprint them is gratefully acknowledged.

This collection was completed with the assistance of a 1987 Creative Artist Award from the Michigan Council for the Arts.

NLM

Contents

PART ONE: OCTAVIA

Another Landscape 15

Prologue 16

I. Copper Earth

Genesis 20
Oklahoma Territory 22
Cottonwood Creek 23
Lawrence, Kansas 24
Teacher 26

II. Dear "Son"

Langston High School 28
Refinement 29
Mama 30

III. Red Dust Blowing

Talk 32
A Mighty Rocky Road 33
Another Autumn 34
Wedding 35
Drexel Street 36
Desert Song 38

IV. Changes

Letters to Two Brothers 40
Mrs. Morris 44
Return 45
Letter from Papa 46
Reconciliation 48
Toward Eternity 49

V. Nightfall

    Missouri   52
    Rescue to Virginia   53
    Bedside Visit   54
    At the River's Brink   55
    Message   57

VI. Homing

    Visit to Guthrie   60
    708 South Second Street   61
    Ladies of the Class of 1920   62
    Greenwood Cemetery   63
    At Rest   64

Epilogue   65

PART TWO: OTHER NEW POEMS

Black Poet   69
Our Gardener   70
"The Sun Do Move"   71
Soon I Will Be Done   72
"Ten"   74
Kujichagulia   75

On Corcovado Mountain   76
At Midday   77
Remember Bahia   79

The Last Happy Day   80
Ash Wednesday   84
Images   85

October Lament   86
Memorial   87
Twice a Child   88
Lifeline   89

Signature   90
Old Shoe   91
Without Condition   92
No Choice   94

Jogging at the Health Club   95
In Autumn   96
Letting It All Hang Out   97
Ceremony   99

Photographs
Family History   *110*
Descendants

Part One
Octavia

Another Landscape

In another landscape
I touch my feet to the roof
of an old house.
I settle in to taste
the red clay earth,
hold gently to the ruined shingles
fragile as memory.....

Nearby a train chugs
toward Topeka.
The dust it disturbs
filters through an open window.
A boy brushes a fleck of it
from his eye. A cinder
imbeds itself in the rice
on his dinner plate.

After the table is cleared
I follow your footsteps
through oppressive heat
to the little wooden bridge nearby
as fireflies flicker
and gathering darkness drowns
your muffled sighs
in the crystal creek.

In another silence, my tongue savors
untold complaints.
I spread my wings and journey
with metaphors of light and shadow
from this old house, abandoned
by years, to a new habitation
I reinvent with words.

Prologue

i.

When as a child I wore your face, Octavia
(three years returned to earth), and christened
with your name, set forth on my own odyssey,

I had no clothing of my own, only
depressive hand-me-downs, frayed remnants
of someone else's outgrown legacy.

My father dressed me in your skin,
and such a garment, woven of his fabrication
of a second chance, was not to be discarded easily.

ii.

Gagged on emulsions, tonics, and home remedies
contrived to save me from your early death,
I was injected with your blood. Your spirit
hovered above me like a constant cloud
threatening disaster.

Having escaped your first name
(too poignant a reminder of your brother's grief),
I was still branded with the second,
tormented by chastisement for your careless ways.

iii.
We were sixteen, and your girl-round face
stared from my mirror. Your long curl
fell over my shoulder.

The smouldering coals of your eyes
ignited mine.

iv.
How your rebellious words
flung from my mouth
must have grieved my father!

Yet his transcendent love
for both of us
always forgave.

How could he not remember
planting the seed that sprouted
into weeds that choked out my identity?

"You outgrew the likeness," he told me,
but by then, it was too late.
Reincarnated in my blood,
you were determined not to die.

v.
Your flesh was bonded to my bones,
my feet shod in your stylish
high-buttoned shoes.
Early discontent creased my forehead
with your frown. Your spirit immersed me
and I sank down and down, swirled
in the whirlpool of your eyes,
and drowned . . . .

I.
Copper Earth

Genesis

I.
She from 1866 Victoria,
he from 1856 New Orleans—
Cherokee/Black, French/Spanish/Black—
they came together to make a family.

Through Texas, Arkansas, Kansas, Missouri
they moved, pursuing stability,
dignity, honor, and excellence
in service.

In spite of history's chains.
They came.

II.

And you, Octavia,
firstborn in Waco, Texas in 1885,
the choicest plum on your father's tree:

How did you reconcile that oak piano
that dwarfed your family's temporary little homes
with the sun-bloated hours you worked in cotton fields,
thorns pricking your fingers, blood mingling
with your tears (your mother kissing the wound,
sending you back to earn your share
of coins the family needed to pay another bill)?

How measure your father's college education
against your mother's endless battle
with despair?

How did it feel to live in
the wilderness of those days,
wanting to come out,
wanting to be,
wanting to *be ready*
to walk in Jerusalem just like John?

Oklahoma Territory

A wilderness:
A barren place
a place of chalky skies
of autumn wind and furies
red dust blowing
across the open plains
of discontent.

Autumn, 1902
708 South Second Street
Guthrie, Oklahoma Territory

22

Cottonwood Creek

Cottonwood Creek is rising,
it is rising again. The dying sun
burns a hole through the opal sky.
Heavy air smothers the copper earth;
dark furies churn the waters.

There is no time to wait for Mama's return.
Half-dry laundry must be taken down from the line,
piled into a basket and placed on the highest shelf.
Your voice trumpets orders to the others.

Strip the beds! Stack the mattresses and covers
on top of the piano! Gather the shoes
and coats! Load them on top of the bedclothes!
(As an afterthought, you add the towel
you have been working on to the pile.)

Collect some changes of clothing.
Be ready to move to higher ground
the minute Mama gets back.
But she must hurry.

In a few days when you return,
Robert will help Marcellus push the piano
onto the L-shaped stoop to dry.
You and Ethel will help Mama
wash down the walls and disinfect the floor.
The things that cannot be redeemed
will have to be discarded.

It will be weeks before the sun's benevolence
dries out the farthest corners of your lives.

Lawrence, Kansas

I.
The basic preparation that normal school would give
was not enough. You yearned for deeper learning,
more for yourself than for the children
you would teach.

Evenings by lamplight in the house on Alabama Street
where board and lodging were provided,
your books were doors of challenge
that would forever open outward now.

Showers of light revived your parched spirit.
The sudden energy of sun electrified your mind.

Autumn, 1905
Lawrence, Kansas

II.
"I'll try to be in Guthrie a few days
early in June," Papa writes.
"I am going to see Octavia graduate
if I must borrow the money to go.
She needs to be commended for her push
and perseverance, and I don't feel
that I can ever do too much for her."

February 15, 1909
Hot Springs, Arkansas

III.
Before you put your cap on, you pause
to smooth an errant strand of hair.
Your baccalaureate gown is opened
to reveal the new white dress,
bow at high collar, that represents
many weeks of sacrifice.

For years, Papa will show your photograph
to friends, boasting of your degree as if
his meager contributions had accomplished it.

June 9, 1909
University of Kansas

Teacher

Hatless, you trudge through alabaster days
   over the railroad tracks
   raised above the level
   of all but the severest floods
to your fifth grade class at Lincoln School
   raw winds biting your naked fingers
   dust searing your eyes.

The furnace is slow to heat
and the only light available
comes through the windows.

   Mama's first grade classroom
   on the floor below
   is even colder, but by ten o'clock
   both will be quite comfortable.

The sweet, high voices of children
   cheer you.
The adoration in their eyes
   warms the dismal atmosphere.
You touch your light to their dark lamps.

Winter, 1909-10
Guthrie, Oklahoma

II.
Dear "Son"

Langston High School

Dear Son,
My school was doing well until three weeks ago
when mumps, measles, and chicken pox broke loose.
Many high school pupils have been out,
but I hope for their early return.

A young Mr. Johnson is rooming where I am.
He seems to have much correspondence with Ethel.
Do you know him?

Hot Springs is on a boom for visitors.
The city is fast filling up with strangers.
My duties as principal seldom permit me
to take advantage of the colored bath house.

Hope you will continue to do well.

Your father,
Frank C. Long

Feby. 15, 1909
Hot Springs

Refinement

My dear Marcellus,
I commend you for the stand
you are taking for Christ
and your determination
to enter the ministry.
I am happy to know
that you have been licensed to preach
and are now at Union. You might send me
the catalogue and allow me to read it.

It is further hoped that you will become
a cultured preacher, refined along all lines,
and not the whining, moaning, and whangdoodling
"befo' de war" variety. Let your education
count for something.

I preach myself once in awhile,
and I am always dignified
and try to let my hearers know
that I am somewhat trained and learned.

Strive to go to the front as a scholar,
pulpit orator, and public man at affairs.
You must educate the people
and not get down to their level.
Write soon and keep me informed of your progress.

Papa Long

Feby. 11, 1910
Hot Springs

Mama

Dear Son,
I am up now but not able to work.
I gave up my school two weeks ago.
Most of my salary last month
went to pay someone for teaching in my place,
doctors' bills and medicine.

I'll get the girls to send you a few dollars
to help you. You got the two dollars
that was sent you first of this month.

I am thankful that I have helped prepare you children
so that you are able to help yourselves,
and if I am oblige to stop work for awhile
I shall feel that you all need not suffer.
Octavia and Ethel have done what they could
since I have been sick. I hope I shall soon
get back my strength.

From your devoted mother.

May 25, 1910
708 South Second Street
Guthrie

III.
Red Dust Blowing

Talk

The sky darkens to a magenta
mirror of your rage. Impossible to stay
in this provincial town, neighbors' eyes
gobbling up your Sunday rides with company
unchaperoned in open carriage.

Letters from Elias beckon you.
A school in Washington may have an opening
after Christmas. By then, there will be no one
left at home but you and Mama,
she clucking her disapproval,
lecturing you on propriety.
Why linger here in loneliness?
Go where the air of freedom
cleanses away despair.

Late summer, 1910

A Mighty Rocky Road

Dear Son,
I am so concerned about you.
It takes all a person can do
to make it these days.
It's a mighty rocky road
up the path of right
and hard to climb.
It takes the guidance
of the holy spirit to take you through.
Man nor angels can't do it
and friends can't.

Oh, my dear son, I do hope you may soon begin
to learn human nature better
and to understand how people use deception.
The world no longer offers truth,
justice and protection to the right,
the earnest and faithful. All must suffer.

I hope the Lord may make you strong
and that you may go forth in this wicked world
as a light for our people.

Oh, do you know the situation? Do you observe
how the colored race in many cases
is going downward? Just think how some men
are making a living by selling out
and destroying the race.

Your devoted mother.

Sept. 30, 1910

Another Autumn

Gray.
Gray wind.
Gray sky.
Gray particles of air
clogging your nostrils,
your life.
The chalky nothingness of gray
dull as your tarnished dreams:
Onset of another winter.

Late fall, 1910

Wedding

Your sister, pristine as a lily,
marries and moves to Brooklyn.
"We shall all miss Ethel," your mother writes Marcellus,
"I most of all, for she has been
my friend through all my tribulations,
always gentle and kind, never giving me
harsh words to grieve me."

But her leaving has cut you
as with the wind's sharp edge.
Who will now caution you against your brashness
without offending, guide you away from indiscretions
with quiet wisdom? Who will you whisper to
now under the eaves after the lanterns
are out and only the indifferent stars remain?

"Yes, Octavia misses her so much,"
your mother's note continues. "She took her leaving
so hard. Write to her often. Advise her
to go to Sunday school and church. Warn her
against her tongue and temper, her hasty
and unkind words. But don't let on
I mentioned anything to you."

November 27, 1910
202 South Drexel Street
Guthrie

Drexel Street

My dear Son,
Your long looked for letter came yesterday,
much to our joy and pleasure.
Of course I am not well but at work
and trying to keep up,
but sometimes I almost give out,
but I must try to keep on going
at least till someone else can take hold
and carry on.

I got this place in order that it might belong
to all of you children
and that all of you might pay for it
so that in the future
you might have a little piece of property
to live in or to be divided among yourselves.
I see no way now to get help
only what Octavia can do.

I want Robert to come out there
as soon as he can, but I am not able
to send him now. I had big Drs. bills,
then I have a big bill from Ethel's wedding.
You know there was no one to give her a string
but Octavia and me.

I long to see the day I can rest.
I have worked and worked till now
I am just worked down and played out,

but how can I bear to see my children
have to take a back seat and come up short.

I hope we all may meet again with Ethel
in some near future day.
Write to her and Mr. Johnson.
He asked about you several times.

Your loving Mother.

202 South Drexel Street
Guthrie

Desert Song

Years in the desert have left me thirsty
and alone. No oasis calls me. My mouth is full
of the taste of sand. I am convinced I will die
of dehydrated dreams.

The pungent odor of rain teases my nostrils
with unkept promises. My tongue swells.
It is always high noon, and there is no tree
to cast a shadow. I have felt

the underground rumbling of trains,
but where is the station where I may get on board?
I long to ride away from here before the talons
of vultures can tear apart this rotting flesh.

IV.
Changes

Letters to Two Brothers
(Virginia Union University)

Dear Son,
Received yours of recent date announcing
your brother's arrival. Am glad to know
you both are doing well.

I had a card this morning from Octavia.
She had just been in Washington 12 hours
when she wrote it. I am expecting
a good long letter from her soon.

Take good care of Robert. It might be best
to let him have your job and you
find something else.
Let me hear from you.

Your affectionate father,
F.C. Long

Feby. 12, 1911
Hot Springs

Dear Rob,
Well, you two boys are together now.
You must make the most of opportunity.
Try to be satisfied. I am real glad
you and Sister decided to leave Guthrie.
It is such a dismal place.

I have had a short letter from Sister.
She likes Washington very much.
The school, she says, is a beautiful place.

Work hard, and write us when you can.
William wishes kindly to be remembered to you.

Your loving sister,
Ethel

February 23, 1911
Woodhaven, N.Y.

My dear Robbie,
I am better now and feeling pretty well.
The weather is very disagreeable,
the cause of so much sickness now.

How are you getting on? Do your best
to be contented. Remember things cannot be
always as we desire, but we can't lose time complaining.
You must have more courage. Strive toward a high
and honorable station in life. Do not be classed
with the slothful and mediocre. Work and depend
upon yourself.

I am sending $3.50 for you to buy some shoes.
Octavia said she is sending some money too.

Well, they are going to bring the capital
back to Guthrie, so they say. They are beginning
to look for a place to put the furniture.

You must practice your music all you can.
You will be glad some day for your piano training.

Love and kisses from your dear Mother.

March 28, 1911
Guthrie

My dear Son,
How I do miss all you children.
How far are you from Octavia?
What is the fare to Washington?
Can't you go there some Friday evening
to see Octavia? Do so if you can.
She would feel better if she could see
some of you all.

Take care of Robbie. Make him keep on
plenty clothes. He better wear
his flannel underwear. Pneumonia
is so bad this time of year.

Your most devoted Mother.
Mrs. Sarah E. Long

P.S. Here is a piece of Ethel's wedding dress.
Keep it to look at.

Mar. 28, '11
Guthrie

Mrs. Morris

Not like your sister's wedding, properly
announced, reported fondly in your mother's letters
detailing everything: a list of gifts, the guests,
a piece of fabric from her bridal gown,
the long train ride to Xenia, then on to Brooklyn.

From you, only a letter to your brother
in seminary in Virginia. "I have intended
for a week to write you. Not feeling very well,
I have procrastinated. Mr. Morris came up to New York
while I was there, and we were married Sunday, June 25th.
His father, in Philadelphia for the Baptist Alliance,
came over and performed the ceremony. Rev. Jernagin
from Oklahoma City came with Rev. Morris.
We had a very pleasant time.
Mama and Elias wish to be remembered to you."

Your wedding dress is lovely, the veil
a filmy coronet gracing your silken hair,
but your head tilts with a suggestion of defiance,
and your eyes are sharp as a dare.

July 6, 1911
200 N Street, N.W.
Washington, D.C.

Return

Whatever lure of freedom
that other world held out to you
turned false as thinly plated gold.
There is no hiding place
down here, and no escape.

Marriage mysteriously ended,
you return to Guthrie
and your maiden name.

The missing pages that could reveal
the truth are lost forever.

Late summer, 1912

Letter from Papa
(324 East Grant Street)

My dear Octavia,
I am pleased to find you
settled again in Guthrie
conveniently across the street
from the new high school
where you will teach.
It is most kind of Sergeant
and Mrs. Green to share their home
with you. Be assured that my hope
for your success and happiness
is constant as the sun.

It is only because I care
for you so much that I now caution you
about your careless speech.
Lately your usage has not been
commensurate with your training.
You are exposed to the criticism
of others who have less education.
If you are not careful, you will hear
of these complaints, and they will sound
unpleasant to you. I would advise
that you take up some good grammar text
and study it until
you have mastered the rules.

Another caution: Make it a point
to avoid involvement in the affairs
of others. Do not let your tongue speak

before your brain considers.
Failure to take this advice
will only cause you further grief.

I hope your mother is resting easy
and feeling better than when I left.
Look in on her
as often as you can.

Write to me at your convenience
and keep me informed of your progress.

Your affectionate father,
F.C. Long

September 10, 1912
Hot Springs

Reconciliation

What were you seeking? What did you find
that wasn't there before?
Had the times changed so much as to accept
your independent spirit,
or had you simply learned to juggle
the images of model teacher,
lady, and liberated woman before your time
without dropping any of the balls?

Weren't you more at peace then
with yourself and with the world around you
than you had ever been before?

Maybe you were disappointed
that life was not a challenge anymore,
only a cool and solid nugget
you could tuck inside your pocket
and secretly feel with your hand whenever
you needed reassurance.

Something you could take out and look at
late at night when you were alone
like a rare and costly jewel.

Maybe that was enough.

1912-1917
Guthrie

Toward Eternity

The live coals of your eyes
smoulder like those of a tired mare
that has finished her journey.

Your hair's proud pompadour
is flat now as the Oklahoma plains.

Fashion has replaced your proper
high-collared dress of dark, ribboned brocade
with flimsy cotton, relaxed at the throat.

Often now you are too weary to meet
with after-school piano students.
Suddenly you are lonely,
your mother four years dead
and no one left in Guthrie
whose blood you share.
You worry the hours away
endlessly tatting towels
to make sleep come.

Mrs. Green is concerned about your cough,
your lack of energy. You open books of poetry
and read deep into the night.

In your broken sleep, you dream of horses
scaling the tops of houses. When
do you first suspect the direction
of their hooves?

1918
324 East Grant Street
Guthrie

V.
Nightfall

Missouri

Robert's wife will not come near you.
Reluctantly she has agreed
to let you stay in the drafty barn,
but she begrudges you what meager comfort
such shelter can provide.

The isolation of a leper plagues you
like flies buzzing around an open wound.
You long for a tin cup of water
to cool the fever of long Missouri midnights.
You welcome the company of bats,
study with awe the symmetry of spiders' silk.

When the weak morning light finally
leaks through the planks, you drift
into deranged shadows of sleep.

Your brother stands by silent and sad.
Physician to others, he is helpless to cure
his own subordination to his wife's
indomitable will.

1919
St. Louis, Missouri

Rescue to Virginia

It was as if intoxicated demons
raged across the land
spewing their wrath into charged air
the day Marcellus came
and found you in such circumstances.

Only his pain was more intense,
for you had been his strength and inspiration,
his symbol of courage and improbable achievement,
and you had always felt for him a special bond
of tenderness and understanding.

Rescue you he must!
Without a map to guide him,
he began the only journey
love and duty would let him travel.

December, 1919
St. Louis

Bedside Visit

"Marcellus, bring him to see me.
He need not come too close, but let me see
your firstborn child before I die."

Blood thicker than the red clay of Oklahoma,
stronger than the marriage bond
prevails. In spite of his wife's pleas
and protests, your brother dresses the boy
in clean bright rompers
and takes him to your bedside.

His wife, fearful for the child,
resentful of this test of loyalty,
screams in frustration, beats her fists
against the door. She thinks she may lose
the baby she is carrying.

It will be a week
before she speaks to him again
with tenderness.

January, 1920
Charlottesville, Virginia

At the River's Brink

"Come, Miss Octavia, let me plump your pillow
and prop you up awhile. You need to take
a little nourishment. Rev. Long will be here soon
and he will want to see his sister
with some color in her cheeks."

Even the slightest movement brings on
another spell of coughing. The neighbor
in whose home you are receiving care
hands you a clean rag. In a few minutes
she will fold the bloody sputum inside,
careful to touch only the dry edges,
and take it to the yard to burn.

Once quiet, you are too tired
to take the hot broth she has brought you.
All you want to do is sleep, and yet
you are afraid to close your eyes
for fear you will not open them again.

When he comes, he will stand near the door
fidgeting with his hat. How he will long
to hold you and kiss your fevered forehead,
but he has been cautioned. His wife and children
need him. He must not jeopardize
his health and theirs by touching you.

Both you and he will guard against
memories of shared childhood, thistles in the fields,

conspiratorial mischief. He will make
light talk, attempt a humorous remark or two.
Before he leaves, he will have a word of prayer,
risking his tentative emotions to invoke
God's intercession and His blessings on you.

Your death will be the keenest test of faith
that he will ever know.

February, 1920
Charlottesville

Message

The whimpers of his week-old son
rescued your brother from fractured sleep
just as the message came: "Come!
She is fading fast. Come quickly!"

March 23, 1920
Charlottesville

VI.
Homing

Visit to Guthrie

Trunks full of brown letters,
brittle photographs,
and towels with tatted edges—
fragments of conversation heard in childhood—
a family Bible—notes hastily scribbled
in an old man's hand:

Because of these I came.

And that old piano that traveled
from Guthrie to Wilberforce
to New Rochelle to Detroit,
symbol of those whose fingers touched it,
whose voices rose above its dissonance
and made a melody:

Because of this I came.

May, 1987
Guthrie

708 South Second Street

A slim tree leans against this ruined house
forlorn and silent now, grieving
for long dead children.

The base is gutted by the curiosity of squirrels.
Gray siding falls away. Boards blind the windows
that once looked out on boys tossing a ball.

Around my face insects buzz coded messages
I cannot decipher. A kitten
peeps at me through the back fence.
Only a few short yards away
the rusty waters of Cottonwood Creek beckon.

Long ago the overflowing Cimarron River
reddened the gurgling creek. Disturbed now
only by a sluggish breeze, the waters murmur:
"Listen. Her footsteps often sounded
on the little bridge above me.
Her tears melted into my ripples.
If you are searching for her spirit, listen.
Be still and listen to my song."

May, 1987
Guthrie

Ladies of the Class of 1920

On sagging porches, in wheelchairs, in garden swings,
across unpaved streets from grazing cattle,
I find them—Miss Minnie Tillman;
your friend Dorinda's sister, Beulah Wigley Smith;
Loletta Finley; Katherine Jackson Chadwick;
Vivian Hamilton—holding their own at 85.
"Octavia Long was my high school English teacher,"
they all tell me.

And one, ten years their senior,
puffing on a slim brown cigarette,
nails lacquered wicked red,
steady on high-heeled shoes:
"I knew the whole Long family.
Marcellus tried to court me
but I was too young for him."
And I: "Marcellus was my father."
"You must send me your picture."
I promise Ollie Matthews Fried I will.

Your photo in the Faver High School yearbook
of 1917. (Next year would be your last
before illness removed you to Missouri.)

"You look a lot like her. She was about
your size and color. You have her eyes."

I touch your ring of tiny pearls
that fits my finger still
and feel your hand closing over mine.

May, 1987
Guthrie

Greenwood Cemetery: Section MKG

I have come home to a land where
I have never been before

seeking to place missing puzzle
pieces in symmetry.

Grandfather whom I never knew,
can you feel my footsteps

over your grave? Do you approve
my proper grammar as

I whisper questions with no
answers among these weeds?

A sudden downpour anoints this
forgotten plot of earth.

The soil drinks deep awakening
your spirit. Is it your

voice the clouds bear? "Octavia, you've
come. At last you have come."

Hot Springs, Arkansas
May, 1984

At Rest

I searched for you and found you.
Now I leave a yellow rose
of remembrance on your grave.
Soon enough I will return
to join you in this sod, but
till then, I exorcize you
from my spirit, old skeleton
rattling around all these years
in my skin. Now be at peace.
Rest. Rest now. And so will I.

August 29, 1987
Mt. Olivet Cemetery
Richmond, Virginia

Epilogue

........I heard somebody call my name
and I rose slowly through murky depths
of otherness until I reached the surface
and emerged at last into unfamiliar sunlight,
breathed the free air and swam
safely to shore.

Part Two
Other New Poems

Black Poet
(In memory of Langston Hughes)

How we are nourished by
his every word!
How we roll it around
in our mouths
like ripe fruit
wishing to savor it long,
digest it slowly
into our selves!

He has cut down our harps
from drooping willows
and handed them back to us
commanding us to sing.
Our blues voices
he has amplified into
anthems of praise,

gathered fragments
of our splintered dreams,
kneaded them together
in healing hands and cried,
"Be whole!"

Surely it is his
nimble fingers still
that teach us how
to harvest ripe figs
from thorn trees
that were supposed to die.

Our Gardener
(For Gwendolyn Brooks)

You are our gardener in a land of blight.
You enrich arid soil, purify
polluted air, shower on us benedictions
of sun and rain.

Because of your hands' gentleness,
fragile stalks grow strong,
healthy roots burrow deep
expanding their power.

Strengthened by your spirit,
nurtured by your caring,
we blossom for you, dear sister.
We give you our sunflower faces
as a token of our love.

"The Sun Do Move"

Who wouldn't believe,
who wouldn't,
who wouldn't believe?

Camp meeting outside
the city limits.
Corn-high, the yellow wave
of faith, gushing
on his word.

> And God said . . . .
> > *Preach it, brother!*
> The Good Book reads . . . .
> > *Yes, it do, Lawd, it do!*
> Day climbing over the southeast
> corner of the earth,
> grasping for the truth.
> > *Tell it, John Jasper,*
> > *Hallelujah!*
> All day long, all Sunday afternoon
> the fields outside of Richmond rocking.

Sun melting down like lard
on the griddle of the world,
the hungry square of earth swallowing
it up again.
> *Come, Jesus!*

Who wouldn't believe,
who wouldn't, who
wouldn't believe!

(John Jasper [1812-1893 or 1901], a former slave, accepted the entire Bible literally and, through exhaustive study, was able to "prove" the mobility of the sun and the flatness of the earth. His famous sermon, "The Sun Do Move and the Earth Am Square," drew crowds of worshippers to his church, as well as to camp meetings in the country. So convincing was his sincerity and so powerful his oratory that even those who knew better were convinced, even if only momentarily, of the authenticity of his claim.)

Soon I Will Be Done
"I'm so glad trouble don't last alway."
(Negro Spiritual)

All my life I been waitin
for trouble to pass.

If it wasnt a flood, it was a drought.
If it wasnt the boll weevil,
it was white folks tryin to take our lan.

Soons we built a house big enough
for all the kids, they raised our taxes.

Then Papa died and Mama come to live with us
with all her furniture cause Brother say
we the onlies ones with that much room.

Soon as Son got outa trouble
Suzie come up pregnant.

We was all so proud of Junior when he come back home
from Viet Nam with medals an honors
an his picture in the paper
till the polices gunned him down
robbin a grocery store.
(Leas thats what they told us.)

I use to sing in church
(an truly I did believe):

"Soon-a will be done with the troubles of the worl,
Goin home to live with God."

But I betcha anything
soons I get to heaven
the golden stairs is gonna fall down
and Gods gonna say, "Sistuh Johnson,
see kin you give us a han here."
Sure as anything, I'm gonna be the one
has to build em back up again.

"Ten"

I have become
a sixteenth century
Italian sculpture
in blackface
with hips too broad
and belly corn-
bread-ample, ham-
hock happy

Nobody idolizes
me
anymore
singing me lovingly
lustily (like Sterling)
"sweet-hipted mama
sweet-hipted Mame"

I have
not so simply
grown bountiful and
sometimes wiser than
brothers
chasing illusions
of frail, pale African
queens
with lisping voices
and platinum
corn-rowed hair.

Bo Derrick, the Caucasian star of the motion picture Ten *was erroneously credited by the media with inventing a hairstyle that is traditionally African.*

74

Kujichagulia

All these years corked up in a dank cellar
waiting for someone else's pronouncement
that it is ready to be opened. Some ancient

spirit moves through fermented fruit. The cork
pops. The ground receives libation with wine
determined to declare and name its own vintage.

Kugichagulia: *self-determination* in Swahili

On Corcovado Mountain

High above the sands
of Rio, clouds veil
the impassive face

of the Redeemer.
Momentarily
pale sunlight steals through

seeking refuge in
folds of the stiffly
fluted skirt. Below

in deeper shadows,
in crevices of
precarious hills

crouch faceless squalid
children whom those out
stretched arms will never
hold, never redeem

At Midday
(A birthday wish for Jill)

Woman to woman now, we tell our beads
on the worn rosary of years
together in the same slant of light.
No longer clay and potter,
we are what we have made each other,
your mark indelibly on me
as mine on you.

And so, at midday, I wish you
a taste of cururú and jaca fruit,
aroma of coconut and palm oil,
resonance of agogô bells at Carnival,
your fingers' touch on a berimbau,
and a silver balangandan hung with amulets.

May the *pretos velhos* endow you with their wisdom,
Yansan clear your path of storm and rain,
and Yemanjá protect and guide you
as you sail forever toward Brazilian shores.

CURURÚ: greens cooked with fish, pepper, and palm oil
AGOGÔ: double metal bell played at Carnival and candomblé rites
BERIMBAU: string instrument consisting of a bow, gourd, and
          small stick
PRETOS VELHOS: African ancestor spirits
YANSAN: Yoruba goddess of wind and storm
YEMANJÁ: goddess of the sea

Remember Bahia
(Lembrança do Senhor do Bonfim da Bahia)

Stumbling into someone else's dream,
came to old Pelhourinho.
Climbed the steep cobblestones
where African women hawked their sweet
concoctions in Portuguese.
Entered through narrow doorways
to watch ballooning white skirts swirl
around black ankles, dancing in praise
of Yoruba deities. And in Filinto's art shop,
soothed the carved nailtorn hands
of a writhing Christ. (Beneath scarred ebony feet
entwined in agony, mask of an African
endures with dry impassive eyes.)

At the Church of the Good End,
hung up my home-lost spirit
among the wounded plastic limbs
of those who came to pray for miracles
and left it there.

Stumbled into someone else's dream
and made it mine.

The Last Happy Day
(In memory of Alfred O. Williams [1911-1984]
and Irene Hunter Williams [1919-1984])

JULY PHOTOGRAPHS

1. *The Godchild and Her Daughter*

The prepubescent girl circles her mother's waist
with spindly arms growing too fast for her body.

Behind them a jovial sun dazzles the depths of green
and scarlet in leaves and blood-ripe roses.

Just out of sight, the old pair
whose love is deep-rooted as ancient olive trees
smile at their little girl
now grown to womanhood and mother of the child.

Nobody asks, "Where will tomorrow take us?" Enough
to be together here encircled by a wreath of sunlit love.

We too have grown gnarled together.
We count the common rings
in the trees we have become.
Our roots sink into deep soil
and our bark is impervious
to wind and weather.

2. *The Man*

Cameras catch the sunlight's vigor
dancing in his eyes. In the velvet dark
his face turns like a sunflower to the brightness
he can no longer see. His fingers remember
the soil's rich balm, the profusion of petals—
daylilies and roses—splashed with gold.
His laughter is a deep-throated bird among them.

Suddenly a shadow falls
across his brow, his hair's
cool silver the one
remaining light.

Nine days to doom,
nine days to paradise.
One perfect hour before
the daylight dies.

SEQUEL: THE WOMAN

Summer does not dissolve
to autumn, then winter
but jolts and quakes
as the widow's tears
gush in vain to soothe and mend
the broken earth.

DECEMBER FINALE

1. And then,
   as though his spirit called her
   (but not so full of terror
   and surprise!)

   as though
   he spoke her name
   (but never wishing her goodness
   to deliver her to evil!)

   she was wrenched away.

2. Morning and conversation with a friend,
   interrupted by insistent jangling at the door.
   "The boy is back, says he dropped the lunch
   I packed for him. Claims somebody in a car
   was chasing him. I'd better hang up now.
   Talk to you later."

                          Stealthy fingers rifle
   the open purse. How to confront him, how
   reprimand the audacity of one so frequently
   befriended? Suddenly, raw energy unleashed,
   animal eyes ferocious. Phone yanked from mooring
   by hands no longer boy's but brutal hammers pounding,
   bashing. A single scream for him who can
   no longer hear, whose blind eyes, even if he could
   be with her, would leave him helpless to defend.
   Then the length of rope produced from nowhere,
   whipped into place, stretched taut against tender
   flesh, vulnerable cartilage. The mouth open

gasping for air, the bulging eyes pleading until
the kindness of eternal dark engulfs her.

By what shall we remember you? Not
the eggs spilled on the kitchen floor
or the now rotting meat intended to relieve
his savage hunger. Not your stifled wail
beating forever against our throats, or the sound
of your head bumping down the basement steps—
the congealed blood under the pulp of your face—
the broomstick left protruding from your anus.

Ironic now the photographs in summer's
idyllic garden on the last happy day
we shared. But "nothing worth keeping
is ever lost in this world." Even in *this* world
may the love-deep roots of trees
conquer evil's senseless blight
and the perennial flowering of your memory
sustain us through whatever winter weather
we still may know.

For Melvin Stringer

Ash Wednesday

Christmas gives way to Easter.
In the second month
snow begins its slow dissolve to lilies,
pain to peace. Hope bursts its bonds
through frozen soil.

Earth turns, gray sky ascends to blue
in sure, eternal cycle
of victory over madness, meaning
over despair
as the new Christ rises reborn.

I too will come again
into my own bloom some springtime
when birth and resurrection meet
after the bloodied spear
has struck its deepest blow.

Images

1.
One student (white),
leading a class discussion
of *Native Son*
and running out of things to say,
asked, "How would you feel
if you encountered Bigger Thomas
on a dark street
late at night?"

Another student (black, astute)
countered: "How
would you know it was
Bigger Thomas?"

2.
I pictured him as muscular,
dull-eyed and dense, his sullen scowl,
skin color, maze of hair
and criminal demeanor defining
my most horrendous nightmare.

How can I reconcile
that image
with this tender yellow
boy who could have been
my son?

October Lament
(For Clarence)

Frame angular, skeleton
leaning toward death
gushing dark waves of bile

Face carved
in ebony pain, teeth jumbled
in familial design

Pattern of generations
persistent still in timbre
of God's chosen voice. . . . . . .

> *In open Bible, futile*
> *passages of hope highlighted*
> *green in lifeless hands. . . . . . .*

> Outside the leaves dance scarlet
> and gold. They sizzle in celebrations
> of flame on rain-glanced pavement

> But Brother, your stillness
> hovers over me this crystal day
> like premature icicles

> melting their chill
> upon my wilted spirit
> drop by mournful drop

Memorial

(For the reverend doctors
Clarence M. Long, Senior and Junior)

Father, give them
a small room together
with water running fluid
as their thoughts
into a marble bowl,
where they can probe
the electric air
with morning razors,
their lathered faces sharing
a mirror steamed up
with the sermons
they preach
to each other.

Twice a Child

(For my mother at ninety)

Butterflies fan fragile, filmy wings
in the darkening forest I lead her through,
holding her hand, guiding her trembling
footsteps, buttoning her memory
as I used to dress my dolls
when she was mother
and I was child.
Now overhanging leaves
filter fading gold through shadow
to the damp and slippery ground beneath
as she drifts through the twilight
of a fairy tale whose characters' names
she has forgotten.
And I can only guess what distant bells she hears
tolling at the top of the hill
she climbs on all fours.

Lifeline
(For Malaika)

Over and over again
urging the car reluctantly through panic
slidingcareeningcrashingfalling
blackingoutupsidedown
facedown on upturned ceiling
sensing the hiss of steam the
whispered voices the throbbing eye
the shattered bones . . . .

Every time, that first dread winter after,
when I relived the death I cheated,
forcing myself to confrontation of my fear,
I bent to grasp this memory:

> *You, in the railroad station in Los Angeles,*
> *just learning how to run,*
> *eyes laughing, taking on the challenge—*
> *you stumbled toward me, arms outstretched*
> *to welcome my return.*

Teaching me how
to learn to run again,
Malaika, you rescued me
over and over again.
You gave me back my courage,
connected me with all
I had to live for.

Signature

Messages sing toward you along taut wires,
sizzling across electric feathers of snow.

Without warning, bulbs burst into brightness
all along the highway; sometimes
fire engines clang with metal urgency.

Do little bells tingle you silverly awake
some mornings? Do flints of sunlight
strike against your skin, ignite?
And do you rise then with inexplicable
joy and energy?

I send you messages along taut wires
singing, incendiary. Are you
receiving them? Do you
recognize their signature?

Old Shoe

I'm an old shoe.
I'm made of good leather.
I wear well.

When the new shoe pinches
I'll be here, carelessly
tossed under the bed but waiting
and ready to give relief.

If I had nothing to clothe
I'd lose my shape and go flat.
So put me on. Wear me
in comfort and with ease.

Without Condition

All these years
I have loved you
without condition
of return,

laid my sacrifices
at the altar
of your need.
Spring

never spiralled through
reluctant soil without
my touch, or
summer

surged through sun
and azure wind
without my presence
at your rebirth.

I have wished you
cardinals and lemonade,
lake water stroking your hand,
sunrise,

and songs
my frail voice could not
sing but only
say.

When the first
green leaf turned
scarlet or gold,
I have been

there always.
When winter blanketed
dead leaves in snow, I have
been there.

So what if now
another voice sustains you,
another hand teaches you what
love means?

It's all right, it really is
all right because

I have loved you all
these years
without
condition of return.

Suggested by "Through This Same Garden,"
a short story by Rachel Winter

No Choice

All that I want of you I take.
It's not your privilege to offer or withhold.

The sun climbs the morning and has no say
in who receives its benediction.

Rain falls and can't select
who is to be refreshed.

You are. I take from you
all that I need.

Jogging at the Health Club

In mirrors reflected in mirrors
I meet myself coming and going,
I leave by the same doors I enter,
the rooms I inhabit instantly vanish.

Through doubled eyes I watch my face dividing,
colliding with itself: splintered
selves casting many-colored prisms
in all directions at once, folding
into themselves, reappearing,
devouring, multiplying . . . .

On such a runway do I recognize
refractions of my self, accepting
that all things are divisible, that
one's sum of parts is other
than a whole.

In Autumn

In my attic a family of squirrels
scurry through brittle dust.
Their metal claws strike sparks
on the floorboards' bare expanse.

On the first brisk autumn day
their quick feet bring me in
from the cold.

At night I worry over
woodwork being chewed to dust,
caves being carved to shelter
screeching dooms of wind.

But in the morning, when I confront
one creature, wary-eyed but fat and furry
as the neighbor's cat I snuggled azure eons ago,

I wonder how I got along all summer
alone in this silent house
burying acorns of my need.

Letting It All Hang Out

Gray Strands

1. Badge of trial
   and triumph:
   It is mine, I have
   earned it.
   I wear it proudly.

2. There is nothing
   more lovely
   than silver framing
   a face
   of old ebony.

Girdle

1. Don't need this noose
   anymore.
   Won't choke myself with
   someone
   else's brand of rope.

2. Free now to ride
   the waves of
   the wind unbridled,
   to float
   on a crest of cloud.

Liberation

1. For the last time
   undo these
   thirteen fasteners
   of a
   longline, long-lie bra.

2. What if my once
   firm breasts sag?
   My fountain runs full
   and free.
   My children bless me.

Ceremony

"Anyhow," he said, "at this point in your life,
surely you don't want any more children,"
the question mark in his voice suspended
like a broken branch afraid of being cut away.

"Of course not," I assured him,
concealing my glee, even
with the scalpel's edge impending.

That evening, dinner alone
with wine by candlelight
and Music for Seasoned Lovers,
and just before midnight:

a ritual burning of my last box
of kotex — flushing of a month's supply
of The Pill down the toilet
in celebration.

The Long children (left to right):
Ethel, Robert, Octavia, and Marcellus

Naomi (left) and Octavia
"... as a child I wore your face..."

Ethel
"...*always gentle and kind* ...."

Octavia

Marcellus

Robert

Marcellus (standing) and Robert in later years

Sarah Long (right) with her first grade class

Sarah and Frank Long

708 South Second Street in 1987
"... forlorn and silent now ...."

202 South Drexel Street, then and now
"*. . . a little piece of property. . . .*"

The Long Family

Franklin (Frank) Cornelius Long was born in New Orleans, Louisiana, probably about 1856 of mixed African, French, and Spanish heritage. Little is known about his family except that he had a brother Robert who died in New Orleans early in 1909 leaving a wife and six children.

Frank was graduated from Leland College (located then in New Orleans on the present site of Tulane University) with close to a 4.0 grade average, in spite of his remark in a letter that he had had no one to help him. His curriculum included mathematics, history, science, philosophy, literature, composition and rhetoric, six courses in Greek, seven in Latin, and three in German. He also studied at the Kansas State Normal School in Emporia, The University of Michigan at Ann Arbor, and the University of Chicago (or Chicago University), eventually earning a master's degree.

A minister whose business card advertised him as a singing evangelist and "the man with a blackboard," he never seems to have pastored a church but spent his adult years as an educator. Moving with his family through Texas, Arkansas, Missouri, and Kansas, Frank taught at a number of schools, from primary to college, and served as principal of several. (He was responsible for the building of at least one and possibly two of these schools.) He served as the first black instructor at Bishop College, located then in Marshall, Texas. City records contained at the Oklahoma Territorial Museum in Guthrie indicate that he was principal of Lincoln School in 1900 and lived on Mansur Avenue between Fourth and Fifth streets. He moved to Hot Springs, Arkansas shortly after that, leaving his family in Guthrie. He apparently never lived with them again but remained involved in the lives of his children. He was principal of Langston High School in Hot Springs (which originally contained primary grades) until 1915 or 1916.

Letters of recommendation from such persons as the mayor of Hot Springs, a member of the school board, and the superintendent of the State of Arkansas Department of Education gave him superior ratings for his character, vigor, educational qualifications, leadership, good name, and community involvement, one indicating that he had spent thirty years in education. In spite of these letters of support, he evidently failed to secure a position as head of the normal school in Pine Bluff and subsequently moved to Memphis, Tennessee, where he continued as an educator and occasional preacher.

Before leaving Hot Springs, his wife having died in 1914, he married Sarah Baker, who worked as an attendant at the white bath houses. She remained in that city during his years in Memphis.

In 1924 he suffered the first of a series of paralyzing strokes, and his wife took him back to Hot Springs where she cared for him faithfully, first at 215 Silver Street, and then, to avoid the payment of rent, at 6 Helem Street, a house owned by her family, until his death on November 15, 1928. He is buried in an unmarked grave in Greenwood Cemetery in a deserted section overgrown with weeds which was once owned by Union Baptist Church, where he was a member, and one or two other black churches. His second wife, who died in 1967, lies beside him.

Sarah Elizabeth Mumford was born June 4, 1866 in Victoria, Texas, of a black mother, who once might have been a slave, and a Cherokee or part-Cherokee father. (There was a high enough percentage of Cherokee heritage that she and her children were awarded government land in the Southwest.) She had at least one half sister who gave birth to two known children, James and DeLois Arthur.

If the notes of her son are correct, she met Frank Long at Leland College. After their marriage, the couple and their growing family seemed constantly on the move, just a step away from poverty. From Independence, Missouri they moved to Emporia, Kansas (where Sarah attended the normal school), and from there to Guthrie, Oklahoma, the most permanent of their various abodes. (It is possible that they lived in Emporia before Independence.)

Left alone with her children in 1901 or 1902, Sarah lived at 708 South Second Street and taught first and/or second grade at Lincoln School. (Copies of her teaching certificates bearing test scores show that she was well qualified.) In 1910 she made a down payment on a house at 202 South Drexel Street, evidently using funds from the sale of her farm in Hugoton, Kansas, but with her health failing and the children starting new phases of their lives in various places, she was probably soon forced to give it up.

A woman of strong determination and courage, excellent character, and high ideals, she was the strength of the family through all kinds of hardship and adversity and was deeply devoted to her children. Her standards were not false but reflected the period and the culture with which she was familiar.

Her last known address was 1002 East Springer Street. It is not known whether she was living alone or being cared for there by friends.

Sarah died in Guthrie on April 21, 1914 and was buried beside her mother in Victoria, Texas, a small wooden cross marking her grave.

Octavia Cornelia Long was born in Waco, Texas on June 14, 1885. She was graduated from a racially mixed high school in 1903. (A handwritten notation at the bottom of her class picture reads "Squins, '03." Efforts to locate the school have so far failed, but it seems likely that she remained somewhere in Kansas after the family moved to Guthrie in order to graduate with her class.) She received her Bachelor of Arts degree at the University of Kansas in 1909 and for about the next two years taught fifth grade in Guthrie. (Her brother's notes identify her school as Lincoln, where her mother also taught, and her sister's school as Douglas, although residence records at the Oklahoma Territorial Museum have the schools reversed.)

In January or early February of 1911, she moved to Washington, DC and taught school there. Guthrie was described by various family members in negative terms, and she had probably found it even more dull and depressing after her sister married and moved away. Furthermore, a Mr. Morris, with whom she had been corresponding for some time, was living there.

On a Sunday in June of that year, on a visit to New York where her sister lived, Octavia and Elias Morris were married in a small ceremony. The officiating minister was the bridegroom's father, the Rev. E.C. Morris, a prominent Baptist preacher and missionary, who had come east to attend a convention. It is likely that the Long and Morris families were acquainted. The couple apparently lived at 200 N. Street, N.W. in Washington.

The marriage was short-lived; whether there was ever a divorce is not known, but Octavia returned to Guthrie in 1912 in time to teach English at the newly-constructed Faver High School, probably the first black high school in Guthrie. She lived across the street from the school at 324 East Grant Street in the home of a couple who were close friends of the Long family. (Her mother, in failing health, was living at the Springer Street address.)

Although she dated a Bill Martin, Octavia did not remarry. She continued to teach, her photograph appearing in the 1917 Faver High School yearbook, until illness cut short her career. Around late 1918 or early 1919 she went to Missouri to live with her brother Robert and his wife Shirley. When her other brother discovered the conditions under which she was living, he removed her to Charlottesville, Virginia, where she died of tuberculosis on March 23, 1920. She was laid to rest in the family plot newly purchased by her brother in Mt. Olivet Cemetery in Richmond, Virginia. The marble headstone lists her maiden name.

Ethel Elizabeth Long was born in Waco, Texas on June 4, 1887. She was graduated from Topeka (Kansas) Training and Normal School, where she met William E. Johnson, an instructor in business and commerce. According to her brother's notes, she taught second grade at Douglas School in Guthrie. Along with her father, she attended "the Chicago University" for twelve weeks in the summer of 1910 studying music and other subjects.

On November 9, 1910, she and Mr. Johnson were married at the family's newly acquired home at 202 South Drexel Street. The wedding seems to have observed all the rules of propriety although it is not known whether her father was present. The couple left Guthrie to visit the bridegroom's mother at 514 East Main Street, Xenia, Ohio, where additional gifts and another reception awaited them. Ethel's letter from there describes the train journey and hotel restaurants along the way where, at William's suggestion, they "passed" in order to avoid the inconvenience and degradation of Jim Crow facilities.

The newlyweds settled at 1019 Union Avenue, Ozone Park, Brooklyn (later listed as Woodhaven), New York, where William entered government service at the navy yard. Three sons were born of this union, Harold Eugene, Kenneth Lowell, and William, Jr.

The family later moved to the campus of Wilberforce University in Ohio where William held a position of custodian of buildings and grounds for more than forty years.

Ethel eventually went blind from inoperable glaucoma but adjusted well to this inconvenience, still able to do her household chores. She died in Xenia, Ohio on July 13, 1965 and is buried there. Her descendants include three sons, five grandchildren, and six great-grandchildren.

Clarence Marcellus Long was born in Victoria, Texas on August 25, 1888. He was baptised in 1897 in Emporia, Kansas by the Rev. S.S. Jones, who remained his spiritual father for life. (Rev. Jones founded the First Baptist Church in Guthrie in 1899, where the Long family were members.) Called Marcellus by family and friends, he completed college preparatory and printing courses at Bishop College and taught printing there while still a student in late 1906 or the following year. Notebooks containing some of his "orations" written at Bishop reveal a keen intellect and an excellent foundation in composition, history, and classical literature. Oklahoma Territorial Museum records indicate that he worked as a printer for *The Oklahoma Safeguard,* possibly a black weekly newspaper, from 1908 to 1910.

A letter from a friend during his Bishop years refers to his decision to enter the ministry. He was licensed to preach in Langston on May 20, 1909. In spite of his father's initial discouragement, "Son" arrived at Virginia Union University in Richmond in January or February of 1910, wearing a summer suit and with only twenty-five dollars to his name. He petitioned the president for any kind of labor in exchange for his expenses and was permitted to work his way through a three-year course in theology in two and a half years. After being ordained, he supplemented his meager income by preaching at various churches in the country, including one in Waverly, Virginia, and working in Cape May, New Jersey during the summer. (When his brother arrived the following year equally destitute, he again petitioned the president on his brother's behalf with the same success.)

After graduation, he married Maude Salena Hilton of Richmond on September 3, 1913, and began a sixty-three-year career as a clergyman. His first church was Third Baptist in Hampton. He later served as pastor of First

Baptist Church in Charlottesville (1914-1921), where two sons, Clarence, Jr. and Wilbur Franklin, were born, followed by Bank Street Baptist Church in Norfolk (1921-1925), where a daughter, Naomi Cornelia, was born.

While pastor of Calvary Baptist Church in East Orange, New Jersey (1925-1937), he earned his Bachelor of Arts degree at Upsala College, where he was valedictorian of his class, and his Master of Arts in church history at Drew University in Madison. Virginia Union University conferred upon him the Doctor of Divinity degree on June 5, 1929. During the Depression, he taught classes in "Negro" literature and sociology in the federally-sponsored adult education program (Works Progress Administration). His travels included a summer-long visit in 1934 to Europe, where he attended the World Baptist Alliance in Berlin, and to Egypt and the Holy Land.

Marcellus was pastor of Central Baptist Church in St. Louis, Missouri from 1937 to 1942 and of Bethesda Baptist Church in New Rochelle, New York from 1942 until his retirement in 1968. He was responsible for the restoration of Bethesda following fire damage and the building of an attached educational center which now bears his name. He was the first black person to be a member of the New Rochelle Board of Education, a post which he held for ten years.

Following his retirement, he and his wife moved to Detroit, Michigan to be near their daughter. He continued to be in demand as a guest preacher into his eighty-sixth year. He died in Detroit on April 1, 1976 of viral pneumonia. He is buried near his sister in Mt. Olivet Cemetery in Richmond, Virginia. His descendents include two sons and a daughter, six grandchildren, and two great-grandchildren.

Robert Elliott Long Was born in Fort Smith, Arkansas on July 15, 1892. He evidently attended school somewhere outside the city of Guthrie and for awhile worked for five dollars a week at the *Guthrie Daily Leader*. Undecided about career goals, he joined his brother at Virginia Union University at the beginning of 1911, evidently with some financial assistance from his father. He later was graduated from Meharry Medical College in Nashville, Tennessee.

He and his wife Shirley lived in St. Louis, Missouri throughout their marriage except for about four years in Hannibal. He had his own medical practice and served at various times on the staffs of the old St. Mary's Infirmary, People's Hospital, and Homer Phillips Hospital. He continued to volunteer in the clinic at Homer Phillips for three years after his retirement and to practice at his home at 4619 McMillan Avenue until he was eighty-two years old.

In 1958 he published a book of verse, *Levity, Legend, and Sentiment*.

Widowed in 1974, Robert eventually lost his sight to glaucoma and spent his last years in a nursing home, cared for by friends. He died on January 17, 1982, the last of his generation, and is buried in St. Peter's Cemetery in St. Louis. There were no children.

The Descendants of
Franklin Cornelius Long (1956[?]-1928)
Sarah Elizabeth Mumford (1866-1914)

Octavia Cornelia Long
(1885-1920)

- Sylvia Penelope Johnson (1947-)
  (Robert Aulston)
  - Alexander McKenzie Aulston (1973-)
  - Damon Taylor Aulston (1977-)
  - Nicholas Jay Aulston (1980-)

Ethel Elizabeth Long
(1887-1965)
[William E. Johnson]

- Harold Eugene Johnson
  (1912-1981)
  (Camille Cotter Taylor)
  - Harold Eugene Johnson, Jr. (1951-)
    (Cathrine Berry)
    - James Morris Johnson (1987-)

- Kenneth Lowell Johnson
  (1915-1984)
  [Evelyn Belle Lewis]
  - Kenneth Lowell Johnson, Jr. (1944-)
    [Mary Dell Gain Parker]
    - Kenneth Lowell Johnson, III (1971-)
  - Marilyn Elaine Johnson (1949-1978)

- William E. Johnson, Jr.
  (c. 1920 - c. 1972)
  (wife's name unknown)
  - William E. Johnson, III (c. 1950-)

Clarence Marcellus Long
(1888-1976)
[Maude Salena Hilton]

- Clarence Marcellus Long, Jr.
  (1918-1978)
  [Laverne C. Stansberry]
  - Cheryl Marie Long (1949-)
  - Patricia Ann Long (1950-)
    [with Michael Wyatt Tucker]
    - Michael Wyatt Tucker, II (1976-)
  - Clarence Marcellus Long, III (1954-)

- Wilbur Franklin Long
  (1920-)
  (Katie Marie Butler)
  - Kathy Etolia Long (1956-)
  - Karen Octavia Long (1958-)

- Naomi Cornelia Long
  (1923-)
  [Julian Fields Witherspoon]
  - Jill Annette Witherspoon (1947-)
    [Edward Jay Boyer]
    - Liliana Malaika Boyer (1975-)

Robert Elliott Long
(1892-1982)

The name of the parent spouse appears under the descendant's name.

About the Author

Naomi Long Madgett is professor-emeritus at Eastern Michigan University where she was professor in the Department of English Language and Literature for sixteen years. Since 1974 she has been editor and publisher of Lotus Press, Inc. in Detroit.

Her poems have appeared in numerous journals and more than ninety anthologies in this country and abroad. Some have been translated into Dutch, Norwegian, French, and Italian, and several have been set to music and publicly performed.

She has received numerous awards for her poetry and has recorded at the Library of Congress. An essay on her work will appear in the forthcoming volume of *A Dictionary of Literary Biography* on black poets before 1955 (Gale Research Company).